BUSTER POSEY

Tammy Gagne

Mitchell Lane
PUBLISHERS

P.O. Box 196
Hockessin, Delaware 19707
Visit us on the web: www.mitchelllane.com
Comments? Email us: mitchelllane@mitchelllane.com

PUBLISHERS

Printing   1   2   3   4   5   6   7   8   9

A Robbie Reader Biography

Abigail Breslin	Drake Bell & Josh Peck	Miley Cyrus
Adrian Peterson	Dr. Seuss	Miranda Cosgrove
Albert Einstein	Dwayne "The Rock" Johnson	Philo Farnsworth
Albert Pujols	Dwyane Wade	Raven-Symoné
Aly and AJ	Dylan & Cole Sprouse	Robert Griffin III
Andrew Luck	Emily Osment	Roy Halladay
AnnaSophia Robb	Hilary Duff	Shaquille O'Neal
Ashley Tisdale	Jamie Lynn Spears	Story of Harley-Davidson
Brenda Song	Jennette McCurdy	Sue Bird
Brittany Murphy	Jesse McCartney	Syd Hoff
Buster Posey	Jimmie Johnson	Tiki Barber
Charles Schulz	Joe Flacco	Tim Lincecum
Chris Johnson	Jonas Brothers	Tom Brady
Cliff Lee	Keke Palmer	Tony Hawk
Dale Earnhardt Jr.	Larry Fitzgerald	Troy Polamalu
David Archuleta	LeBron James	Victor Cruz
Demi Lovato	Mia Hamm	Victoria Justice
Donovan McNabb	Miguel Cabrera	

Library of Congress Cataloging-in-Publication Data

Gagne, Tammy, author.
 Buster Posey / by Tammy Gagne.
    pages cm. — (A Robbie reader)
 Includes bibliographical references and index.
 ISBN 978-1-61228-458-3 (library bound)
 1. Posey, Buster — Juvenile literature. 2. Baseball players — United States — Biography — Juvenile literature. I. Title.
 GV865.P676G34 2014
 796.357092 — dc23
 [B]
                                                                    2013023055
eBook ISBN: 9781612285160

ABOUT THE AUTHOR: Tammy Gagne is the author of numerous books for adults and children, including *Ke$ha* and *Will.i.am* for Mitchell Lane Publishers. She resides in northern New England with her husband and son. One of her favorite pastimes is visiting schools to speak to kids about the writing process.

PLB

TABLE OF CONTENTS

Chapter One
A Tough Break 5

Chapter Two
Old-Fashioned Values 11

Chapter Three
Working on His Weaknesses 15

Chapter Four
The Move to San Francisco 19

Chapter Five
A True Recovery 23

Career Statistics 28
Chronology 29
Find Out More 30
    Books 30
    Works Consulted 30
    On the Internet 30
Glossary 31
Index 32

Words in **bold** type can be found in the glossary.

San Francisco Giants catcher Buster Posey is shown here during the second inning of a game against the Arizona Diamondbacks on June 7, 2013.

CHAPTER ONE

A Tough Break

It was the top of the 12th inning in a game between the San Francisco Giants and the Florida Marlins. The score was tied, 6-6. Emilio Bonifacio hit a fly ball and his Marlins teammate Scott Cousins began racing toward home plate. When he got there, he crashed into the Giants' catcher Buster Posey.

Seconds later Posey lay in the dirt, twisting in pain. The collision had left him with a broken left leg. He also had torn **ligaments** in his ankle. Cousins had won the game for the Marlins, but Posey wouldn't play for the rest of the 2011 season.

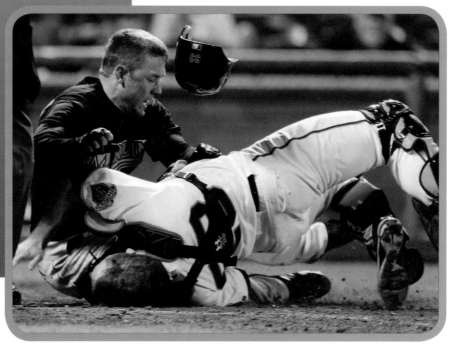

The play that landed San Francisco Giants' Buster Posey on the injured list for the rest of the 2011 MLB season occurred on May 25. In the days and weeks that followed the play, both fans and experts discussed the incident at length. The above photo shows the exact moment when Scott Cousins collided with Posey, breaking his leg.

Fans and sportscasters debated the collision for weeks following the accident. Was it indeed an accident? On his weekly radio show on KNBR, Giants General Manager Brian Sabean called the play **malicious** and unnecessary.

Cousins insisted that he never meant to hurt Posey. He issued a statement saying, "Nobody outside of Buster feels worse about his injury than I do." He also pointed out that the play was "clean and totally within the rules of the game."

Posey shared his thoughts with MLB. com. "You can ask a lot of catchers. You're exposed . . . I think there's a big difference if you're completely in front of the plate just camped out where the runner doesn't really have a choice at that point. But I feel like Cousins had a choice. I feel like he had a choice to either slide or come to me. And he came directly at me."

Posey added that he didn't want Cousins to be seen as a villain. He simply wanted the Major League Baseball Rules Committee to look at the rules for plays like this one. "I feel fortunate it's just my leg that's hurt." He knew it could have been much worse.

Posey planned to return to the game. He knew it would take some time, though. "It's going to be a long, long road to recovery," he told MLB.com. "But it's something I believe I will be able to fully recover from."

Giants right fielder Nate Schierholtz told *USA Today* that Posey's exit was a huge loss. "He's one of the leaders of the team already, and what he brings every day is something you can't replace."

The Giants had started the season with great hope. Just the year before, they'd beaten the Texas Rangers in the World Series. It was the team's first World Series title since 1954. Now the team had lost one of its best players less than halfway through the 2011 season.

Posey holds the World Series Championship trophy on November 1, 2010. He helped the San Francisco Giants win the series against the Texas Rangers in Game Five with a final score of 3 to 1. It was the team's first World Series win since 1954.

Florida State shortstop Buster Posey tags hitter Chad Flack of North Carolina University on May 25, 2006. Fleck was trying to steal second base during the fifth inning of the ACC Baseball Championship in Jacksonville, Florida.

Old-Fashioned Values

Gerald Dempsey Posey III was born on March 27, 1987, in Leesburg, Georgia. He grew up the oldest of Gerald (known as Demp) and Traci Posey's four children. He had two younger brothers, Jack and Jess, and a younger sister named Samantha. Named after his father, Gerald would also inherit his dad's childhood nickname, Buster.

Buster and his siblings were all drawn to sports. Demp had played college basketball, and both Buster and his brothers liked it as well. Right from the start, though, Buster's favorite pastime was baseball. He played nearly every

Buster Posey won both the National League Rookie of the Year Award and the Players Choice Award for 2010. His proud parents Traci and Demp Posey attended the ceremony, which took place just before the Giants' game against the St. Louis Cardinals in San Francisco, California, on April 10, 2011.

position in Little League, and he was very good at all of them.

Buster's parents say he was a very focused kid. He always did his homework and chores without having to be reminded. To this day he never forgets to call his grandparents on their birthdays.

One might say that Buster learned responsibility by example. Demp is now a co-owner in the food distribution company where he has worked for over 25 years. When his kids were younger, he would go into work early each day. Doing so allowed him to take time off in the afternoons to go to their games. In some cases, he also served as their coaches.

Buster's mother is a teacher at a school for kids with discipline and learning problems. She loves what she does. As she explained to the *San Francisco Chronicle*, "If you can keep one kid from dropping out of school and feeling worthless, it's so rewarding."

The Poseys are proud of their eldest son, but no more so than of their other children. Demp freely states that he thinks his most athletic child is his daughter, Sam. He credits Buster's success to his **determination**. "I think he's just the hardest worker," he told the *Chronicle* in 2010.

Posey steps up to bat on April 11, 2012. He served as a pinch hitter in the Giants' game against the Colorado Rockies. San Francisco would lose the game with a final score of 17 to 8.

Working on His Weaknesses

Buster stood out at Lee County High School as both a baseball player and a student. He was a skilled pitcher, hitter, and shortstop for the Trojans. As a junior, he had a batting average of .544 and a 10-1 record as a pitcher. He could also throw a 95-mph fastball. He hit the winning grand slam in the Trojans' state championship game that year.

During the same year, Buster was invited to pitch for the USA Junior Olympic team in Taiwan. Even with all the excitement, he didn't neglect his schoolwork. His mother remembers how he studied calculus on the trip. This dedication paid off. Buster's grades kept him among the top students in his class.

Buster's high school coach, Rob Williams, saw something unique in him. In 2010 he told the *San Francisco Chronicle*, "Most kids want to practice the things that they already do well. The difference with Buster is that he wanted to work on the things that aren't as much fun, where he really needed to improve." College **scouts** were beginning to see something special in Buster as well.

As a senior, Buster continued to grow as both a hitter and a pitcher. His batting average dropped to .462 that year. But he set a school record with 14 home runs. He

enjoyed even more success on the mound. He had a perfect 12-0 record with an **earned run average** (ERA) of 1.06. He was named Georgia Gatorade Player of the Year in 2005.

Graduating fourth in his class, Buster had many options after high school. Scouts from both college teams and major league clubs wanted him. Buster wanted to play college baseball. Even after he made this decision official, the Los Angeles Angels tried to get him to change his mind. He didn't.

He decided to enroll at Florida State University and play for the Seminoles in the fall of 2005. He started out by playing shortstop for the college team. He ended the season with a batting average of .346, four home runs, and 48 RBIs.

By his second season, his coaches had moved him to the position of catcher. Buster met this new challenge the same way he had done everything else in baseball. He practiced.

San Francisco Giants player Buster Posey celebrates his team's World Series win by waving to the crowd during a hometown victory parade on October 31, 2012. The Giants beat the Detroit Tigers in the series.

The Move to San Francisco

Buster's hard work paid off once again as he moved into the position of catcher. He batted .382 his second year at Florida State. He also earned the most RBIs of anyone on the team—65. Buster was named a finalist for the Johnny Bench Award, which is reserved for the best catcher in college baseball. No **sophomore** had ever been a finalist for this award.

In 2008, Buster's batting average rose to .463 with 93 RBIs. His performance was good enough to earn him the Johnny Bench Award. He and his Seminole teammates won 54 games that year. Even more impressive, the San Francisco

Giants selected him as the fifth overall pick in the 2008 amateur draft. Still, he had turned down a professional team three years earlier. Would he accept the Giants' offer? If they wanted him, they knew they would have to make the deal a sweet one.

In August, San Francisco put their offer on the table. They would pay Buster a $6.2 million signing bonus. This was more than they had ever offered any other player. Buster accepted the offer.

Buster married his high school sweetheart, Kristen, in 2009. He had definitely found the right girl. Kristen had helped him prepare for spring training by catching fly balls for him while he practiced. After the wedding ceremony, the couple walked back up the aisle together as the song "Take Me Out to the Ballgame" played.

After playing in the minors for a season, Buster was called up to the major league in 2010. He ended his first season in the majors with a batting average of

After playing in the minors for just a single season, Buster moved up to the majors in 2010. That same year he won two major awards and led his team to a World Series victory.

.305. He hit 18 home runs, 23 doubles, and two triples. He won the award for Rookie of the Year. He also helped his new team win the World Series that November.

Buster Posey played for the National League team in the 83rd MLB All-Star Game. He is seen above warming up before the game at Kauffman Stadium in Kansas City, Missouri, on July 10, 2012. The National League won the game with a final score of 8-0.

A True Recovery

The 2012 season offered Buster a fresh start. His leg had finally healed from his 2011 injury, and he was ready to get back to baseball. Giants Manager Bruce Bochy wasn't so sure. He didn't want to push Buster too much in his first season back with the team. Soon, though, it became obvious that he didn't need to worry. The old Buster had returned in full force.

He led the team with 178 hits, 39 doubles, and 24 home runs. He also played in his first All-Star Game that summer. The biggest surprise would come at the end of the season, though. Buster

Following his 2011 injury, Buster Posey made a thrilling comeback in 2012. He was honored as the 2012 National League MVP that year. He is seen above waving to his fans during the award ceremony, which took place on April 6, 2013.

and his fellow Giants won the National League pennant. Then they swept the World Series against the Detroit Tigers, winning the first four games.

Buster was voted National League Most Valuable Player for 2012. The contest for this award wasn't even close. He received 27 of 32 first-place votes from the Baseball Writers Association of America. Only 10 Giants players in history have won this award. Among them were Willie Mays and Barry Bonds. Buster told the *San Francisco Chronicle*, "To hear my name mentioned with those guys doesn't even seem real."

The Giants know how lucky they are to have him. In 2012 Bochy told the Associated Press, "I'd hate to think where we would be without him. The numbers, they speak for themselves. But also his leadership on this club. We saw what life was without him last year. . . . I don't know a player that's made a bigger impact on a club than what he has on our club. He's

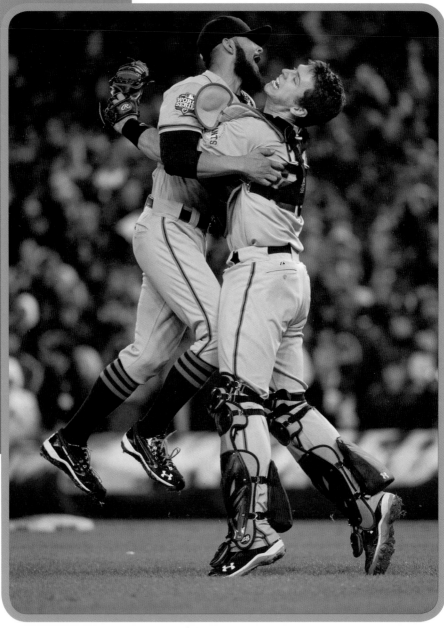

Buster Posey celebrates with fellow San Francisco Giants player Sergio Romo after sweeping the 2012 World Series against the Detroit Tigers. The Giants won the series in Game Four, which was played at Comerica Park in Detroit, Michigan, on October 28, 2012. The final score was 4 to 3.

just a tremendous talent. We're lucky to have him."

Even in the midst of his successful comeback, Buster made time for others. On July 24, 2012, he spent the day with Little Leaguers at the Diamond Skills Camp in Alameda, California. He watched the kids play, shook their hands, and signed autographs.

Buster has come a long way from his days playing high school ball in Georgia. But that willingness to work hard for what he wants is still paying off. In 2011 Buster and Kristen became the parents of twins. Their son Lee Dempsey and daughter Addison Lynn were born while Buster was recovering from his leg injury. No one knows if their children will end up being the next baseball stars in the Posey family, but one thing is certain: If Buster passes his **work ethic** on to them, his kids are sure to be able to achieve their biggest dreams.

CAREER STATISTICS

Year	Team	G	PA	AB	R	H	2B	3B	HR	RBI	SB	CS	BB	SO	BA	OE
2009	San Francisco Giants	7	17	17	1	2	0	0	0	0	0	0	0	4	.118	.1
2010	San Francisco Giants	108	406	406	58	124	23	2	18	67	0	2	30	55	.305	.3
2011	San Francisco Giants	45	162	162	17	46	5	0	4	21	3	0	18	30	.284	.3
2012	San Francisco Giants	148	530	530	78	178	39	1	24	103	1	1	69	96	**.336**	.4
As of 8/26/13	San Francisco Giants	119	419	419	47	127	30	1	14	62	1	1	44	53	.303	.3

G–Games Played
PA–Plate Apperances
AB–At Bats
R–Runs Scored
H–Hits

2B–Doubles
3B–Triples
HR–Home Runs
RBI–Runs Batted In
SB–Stolen Bases

CS–Caught Stealing
BB–Bases on Balls
SO–Strikeouts
BA–Batting Average
OBP–On Base Percentage

CHRONOLOGY

1987   Gerald Dempsey Posey III is born on March 27

2004   Hits the winning grand slam in Lee County High School Trojans' state championship game; invited to pitch for the USA Junior Olympic team in Taiwan

2005   Graduates fourth in his class from Lee County High School; named Georgia Gatorade Player of the Year; enrolls at Florida State University

2006   Begins playing shortstop for Florida State University Seminoles

2007   Moves to catcher position with the Seminoles; named a finalist for the Johnny Bench Award

2008   Wins the Johnny Bench Award; selected by the San Francisco Giants as the fifth overall pick in the 2008 amateur draft

2009   Marries high school sweetheart, Kristen

2010   Called up to the majors with the Giants; wins first World Series with San Francisco

2011   Ends season early due to collision with Marlins player Scott Cousins; becomes father of twins, Addison Lynn and Lee Dempsey

2012   Plays in first All-Star Game; wins second World Series with Giants; named National League MVP

2013   Launches Buster Bash Pro, a mobile game for iPhone and Android

FIND OUT MORE

Books
Funk, Joe, ed. *Comeback Kings: The San Francisco Giants' Incredible 2012 Championship Season.* Chicago: Triumph Books, 2012.

Jackson, Julie, and Scott Jackson. *Great Giants Stories Every Young Fan Should Know.* San Jose, CA: Red Pen Consulting, 2013.

Works Consulted
Associated Press. "Marlin Player Threatened Over Posey." *New York Times*, June 3, 2011.

Chavez, Dustin. "Buster Posey to Appear in Alameda This Summer!" Alameda Patch, April 4, 2012.

Diamond Skills Camp. "San Francisco Giants Star Buster Posey Appeared at Diamond Skills Camp in Alameda, CA on July 24th 2012." http://www.diamondskillscamp.com/proguests/buster_posey/

Dubow, Josh. "Buster Posey Leads Giants Back to World Series." Associated Press, October 23, 2012.

ESPN. "The Giants of Baseball." http://espn.go.com/mlb/playoffs/2010/matchup/_/teams/rangers-giants

Gonzalez, Antonio. "Posey Injured in Brutal Collision in Giants Loss." *USA Today*, May 26, 2011.

Haft, Chris. "Posey Won't 'Vilify' Cousins, Plans to Catch Again." MLB.com, May 27, 2011. http://mlb.mlb.com/news/article.jsp?ymd=20110527&content_id=19642878&vkey=news_mlb&c_id=mlb

Jockbio.com. "Buster Posey." http://www.jockbio.com/Bios/B_Posey/B_Posey_bio.html.

Knapp, Gwen. "Giants Catcher Has Deep Southern Roots." *San Francisco Chronicle*, October 10, 2010.

Schulman, Henry. "Buster Posey is Voted NL MVP." *San Francisco Chronicle*, November 15, 2012.

Seminoles.com. "Buster Posey." http://www.seminoles.com/sports/m-basebl/mtt/buster_posey_9615.html

On the Internet
San Francisco Giants: Giants Kids
    http://sanfrancisco.giants.mlb.com/sf/fan_forum/kids_index.jsp

Sports Illustrated Kids
    http://www.sikids.com/

GLOSSARY

determination (dih-tur-muh-NEY-shuhn)—Willingness to work towards a purpose.

earned run average (URND RUN AV-er-ij)—The average number of runs a pitcher gives up in a nine-inning baseball game.

ligament (LIG-uh-muhnt)—A band of tissue that connects bones.

malicious (muh-LISH-uhs)—Desiring to cause injury or harm.

scout (SKOUT)—A person whose job is to look for talented young athletes for a particular sports team.

sophomore (SOF-uh-mawr)—A student in the second year of high school or college.

work ethic (WURK ETH-ik)—Belief in the importance of hard work.

INDEX

ACC Baseball
    Championship 10
All-Star Game 22–23
basketball 11
Bochy, Bruce 23, 25
Bonds, Barry 25
Bonifacio, Emilio 5
Cousins, Scott 5–8
Detroit Tigers 18, 25, 26
Diamond Skills Camp 27
draft 20
Flack, Chad 10
Florida Marlins 5–8
Florida State University
    Seminoles 10, 17, 19
Lee County High School
    Trojans 15
Leesburg, Georgia 11
Little League 12
Los Angeles Angels 17
Mays, Willie 25
Posey, Addison Lynn
    (daughter) 27
Posey, Gerald (Demp,
    father) 11, 12, 13
Posey, Gerald Dempsey III
    (Buster)
    awards 12, 17, 19, 21,
        24, 25
    birth 11
    charity 27

childhood 11–12
college 10, 16, 17, 19
family 11, 12, 13, 15
high school 15–17
injury 5–8, 23, 24
MLB 4, 5–9, 14, 17, 18,
    19–26
wedding 20
Posey, Jack (brother) 11
Posey, Jess (brother) 11
Posey, Kristen (wife) 20,
    27
Posey, Lee Dempsey (son)
    27
Posey, Samantha (sister)
    11, 13
Posey, Traci (mother) 11,
    12, 13, 15
Romo, Sergio 26
Sabean, Brian 6
San Francisco Giants 4,
    5–8, 14, 18, 19–26
Schierholtz, Nate 8
Taiwan 15
Texas Rangers 8, 9
USA Junior Olympic team
    15
Williams, Rob 16
World Series 8, 9, 18, 21,
    25, 26